Whose World?

for Miriam:
may her world be the best
of all worlds — with love
from Mary

Whose World?

Selected Poems

Mary de Rachewiltz

St. Andrews College Press
Laurinburg, North Carolina
1998

A Note on the Cover Photo:

The window in the chapel of the XI century castle Tyrol is the oldest stained glass found in the region, dated 1330 ca. Above the Madonna is the inscription ALMA MATER and two angels holding candles.

Library of Congress Cataloging-in-Publication Data

de Rachewiltz, Mary 1925. Selected poems / Mary de Rachewiltz—
Laurinburg, NC / St. Andrews College Press
     I. de Rachewiltz, Mary. II. Title

ISBN: 1-879934-55-8

Typeset in Galliard Roman

First Printing: September 1998

This book was to be:

For the friends, students,
and grandsons who share
my Sunday tea.

"But sith one of them has gone out
very quickly from among us"

it is:

"in memoriam eius mihi caritate primus"

JAMES LAUGHLIN

Contents

(Untitled Poems are listed by their first lines)

Nostalgia

A common friend must have liked her
though he is alive no more she is
a beggar always pressed by art
that "strange necessity" and nostalgia
for the *shtetl* where young men played
the jewish harp and women sang
muess i denn muess i denn

Ridiculous this place is
as though it were a Russian orthodox
convent cruel and magnificent where
she takes care of her body
and I take care of her soul
and he takes care of our minds
and both of us worship

The outlook is bleak bleak
the common friend beckons
from the box-wood evergreen
enters my room Melancholia
a blinding whiff of incense
opens the balcony door and brings
dancing steps to our senses

C'est par les odeurs (Céline)
que finissent les êtres
with the fragrance of Zanzibar
with you who have travelled
into a bitter-sweet aura
on attar wings
to the end of the night.

A Journey

I

I write a little book, I
read it to myself, I am
a wormless red apple
eaten unpeeled to the core.
An apple, a book, you-Î
roll up together and write
letters free from angst now that
letters do not get written
or read, letters as people
and books are to burn.

II

A cat so far afield runs
after our train pulling out
and moving into blackness:
a tunnel. The cat has jumped
over the mountain and falls
in front of the moving wheels
the blood of seven lives
spurts from East to West.
Unmoved the young arab sits
on brown velvet. He pulls out
a crumpled letter and joy leaps
to his cheek-bone, cat-paw smiles
curl around his lips and fall
into the dimple on his chin.

III

Her frail figure stood
in the doorway framed
gold against gold,
thus will my man come
tall, so very tall
he cannot cross
the church's threshold.
A gothic George
not comprehending,
leans gaunt on his sword,
no horse, no dragon
to kill. Here eyes do
the swift slaying
and words remain. Mute.

Blood & Sh-t

It started with Isabel
half a century ago
and from a great distance
the dutiful son impeached
devised a new wheel-chair
leaving out the essential hole,
later he said: it's your karma
& Bertolucci has shown
an emperor's excreta
are studied with due respect;
my own children's were honey-
coloured and smelt of sour dough.
Now memory treasures white
gauze and linen fluttering
over snow-dazzle, legs tiny
peach-petalled fingers and toes.
But where the cradle of my brain
stands, a man mops up blood,
his own blood is a man's job
while unendingly here
with intermittent charity
one still tends to an ancient
mother's sh— truly a woman's
karma.

My garden nature is fine
I do not want to change it
each season I plant and sow
what it needs to be a he
and a she growing to feed
and delight us with flowers
pink roses blue zinnias
yellow corn red tomato
orange carrots and green greens
so tender slugs can't resist
dying for them in the long throat
of a single Canada
Mother goose.

Her mind is her
grandfather's battle-
field, her grandmothers
sit tight in her heart,
the body of a fish-
tail moves on cat's-paws
that scratch or soothe.

Snowed-on peach blossom
falls too early prey
to the evil winds,
will not dance mid-air
and bear rounded fruit
but on the ground be
trampled-on rot.

Your wings brushing
against the peaks
take on height
and your joints
a hardness that keeps
the line taut
when the distance grows.
Diamond fulcra
trailing tendrils
no more cut
into the crystalline.
The constancy of rock
has entered your heart
& the bird of fiery tongues
joins heaven and earth
in a white radiance
of tenderness
though men dare not
speak of angels
where love equals mud.

Lois

It was
on a stormy dark night
the chicken long asleep
in the coop along the wall
    by the fire and I perched
on top of them, quiet
with my plate of soup,
when the door blew open,
Holy *Jehssus Maria!*

A *Kornarin* with a bundle
holding a frozen child.

An unwanted babe three months old
had been thrown on a haystack
by a drunken father—the story goes.

Uncalled for you came and left
a big black emptiness none
can fill the silence of your grin.
Your joy was a green felt hat
and the hobby-horse that galloped
with ecstasy when you were six,
unless we count the taste of chocolate
easter eggs arrived by mail
                    when you were three.

That very autumn my childish mother-
love for you caused tears in Venice.
                              Again an empty house
in Venice. I listen to the evening bells.
You are supposed to arrive at the station
                              and find the house.

Wishful thinking never brought you here
though the kind man knew
                              I wanted to show you
the marvel of boats and water.
But you never stepped beyond the furrow
and never saw the green sea.
                              Suddenly
you fell. A grass blade to the scythe
of a mower stronger than you
though your proud overstatement was:
I have always been
                              the strongest mower.

Those who knew you well said:
you felled too many trees.
The wood was dead, you'd shrug and split
and saw away, buzz buzz buzz.
                    Bees swarm
                    to the flowering hibiscus
                    gathering pollen
                    to garner your caring.

Once I knew a tall, grey-haired
literary agent in
New York, 52nd Street.
Suddenly he stands
in his red brick basement
kitchen, while I in mine
improvised Tyrolean
scrape a pot of burnt jam.
He says, opening the doors
of the built-in cabinet:
These are my poems. Taste and see.
Six lines of dainty jam jars
the size of a sonnet,
shimmering hues from amber
to transparent seaweed green,
cyclamen.
                    Does it follow
                    that I should stick
                    to picking,
                    pitting plums,
                    fall asleep
                    and burn?
Provisionally I have salvaged
and installed my old wood-stove
for all the superfluous
paper poems love letters
                    to burn.

To My Night Bird

After a certain age
women know how to court
success.
        They have the words
in their pockets and spend
readily, having bought them
at a reasonable price, no need
to pay exorbitant interest.
But one stopped looking
at the windows with a "Vacant"
sign around N.Y. Grand Central
—there never were any
on Bank Street—courting
a shadowy figure
in a long shimmering
gown of mauve taffeta
while thinking of building
a nest for her night bird.

For T. S.

"Forgive me for pawing your poems"
wrote a woman who knows
that a poem is clutchable
like a bottle of eggnog
handy on the lower kitchen shelf,
its content condensed
in the slanted strip ZABOV
with thick black lettering
on the yellowish yoke.
Only the stemma
in the upper corner
hints with a flourish
of the aromatic wine
from Marsala, Cypress or Malaga
that makes old travellers
dream of sour lemons.

Carol called it comfort food,
something sweet and simple
for the night and it brought
to mind the *Betthupferln*
for two girls a distraught mother
would place on their pillows
to entice them into cold sheets
in wartime when a fragment
of chocolate was heaven.
And a later heaven
                    with a pang.
Along green flat rivers
stopping at random
for a bed & breakfast
to find sweets on the night table.
"Let us worship," he'd say
and she "Yes and forever"
fragments of heaven.
                    So bitter the end
when our differentiated
souls clashed clarity
shattered all preexisting harmonies
from emerald spheres falling
to the ordinary splinter
of that third window pane.

Homespun For Cousin Mary

A tall girl left the *real* Vancouver in
Washington and found a four-leaf clover
in an enclosed castle garden
where she felt equally at home
though wandering why—a *nostos* ?

Now from time to time an entire family
comes visiting from the coast of Maine
and tells of how a grandfather cut all ties
forgetting his native Tyrolean language
while various children have passed on
their knitted cardigans.
                            The tall girl
is a white haired lady who stays
Sappho among grey rock-doves
in the sacred grove a magnet
drawing blood streams from the Pleiades
while poems shuttle in her hands
and weave of skies and water
across the two continents a periplum
                            skirting Nantucket.

Now you have moved into a painted picture
on the wall you have removed yourself
even from that faint trembling of my knees
into a world another man follows your mind
heart moving who once raked leaves
on his own hill of deep Connecticut foliage,
a car races toward your
                    meadow.
The logs in the fire are
                    young birches
grown in clumps.
            Here a bunch of tree women
ancient and aging without hope
of ever returning to foliage and meadow
under blue ridges sink into the bedding
of augean stables without a Hercules.

There is something in this house
needs taking care of. Something
that is not quite in order.
Through rooms and through crevices
light steps rhythmically dance
on the narrow "singing planks"
called the Emperor's watchdogs.
Thieves enter old homes cut up
by roads leading nowhere
that were once a green meadow
binding chapel and tower
to this house. Not to be
a *laudator temporis acti.*
The future still holds
in media matrix the scythe,
the rake, the axe and the sickle
cut into space where once stood
the old barn and a stable.

But how to sing into being
Achilleia's heel planted
on a Tyrolean Noname
under this broad mountain?

Metis, metis, not polu—
but a single-minded know-how:
the grip on the handle
the right twist and elbow grease.
How she swung her hips
into her labours
driving the scythe through
sharp grass, or danced
when turning hay to the sun.
Now a stuttering bald head
would come to tell me
it was merely sex.
Swaddling other people's children,
milking cows and her breast?
Eyes lost on the crucifix
on her deathbed she kissed
her own hands and knees.

Broken Promises are as Good as a Lie

Not caring enough to believe or mis-
believe, Angelman of infinite faith
help me to make believe I do not judge
her fantasies and confabulations.

When greed spreads to the sugar bowl we know
there will be no foundation nor yet land
in Idaho for sheep to graze around
his coat and cane no monument on $
Mountain, what remains is a name engraved
on a dark granite set to holding wall.

Failure can be judged by him alone who
knows the fathoms deep he reached the peaks
he climbed tallied with his aims
                              and no hair split.

Shrinks

All these people have been able
to afford the luxury of a shrink

now their poems are sweet and clear
their problems have all been solved

by an expert testing of dreams—
whereas a mountain goat's entrails

are knotted tight and hard to dis-
entangle when the belly aches

because no amount of echo-
ing will provide the dough

to make bread rise to her mouth &
feed a hungry heart.

Agro-Dolce

Whereas Leoncina somewhere else
waited, little knowing Artemis
and Beatrix through wives and wine
rise past the Arno into heaven.

Changing mid-air to wasp and bee
they carry gold pollen dreams
on spindly legs.
                              Exact
memory spins honey where the light
stands.
            Incipit: here begins
the tale of the Golden Fleece:

Came the Argonauts on a summer's day
in the ninth year of her age,
drones flew from their hives
sheep flocked about the shepherdess
to fend off the thieving knights,
                                              in vain.

They turned her into a waiting
game and drove her past the Arno.
A letter came in mixed grammar and
gender. War came.
                          Leoncina broke
the bars. Lion blood breeds wild
anemones into four-petalled poems
and sings "he'll be coming 'round
the mountain, he'll be coming
to touch my knee." He never came.

                    Late in years
she stormed over the ocean
                              tamed
in his very den dared brush
light lips over thinning hair
searching for the poison pin
to pull, free her knight
                              Unaware.

Incest

Live it down, live it down!
Said the old queen, Windsor
or no Windsor, Pound or
no Pound.
　　　　King Arthur was
my Merlin
　　　　shot from the sky.

E il Poeta stava per divenir pazzo
and his child also.
　　　　　　All the while
by the blue grotto
among Tatiana's lotophagoi
the mother was reclining.
　　　　"God what a woman!"
His sister had asked for a rein-
carnation to continue their games.

Nor yet in anger beauty lies,
not in the flaunting of courage
toujours le beau geste
    to keep the stage.

The *lógos filalethés*
turned out to be a lie
anyway in the light
of madness God's folly
wanting perfection after the carnage
"Not because I have
    but because I try to achieve"
patience. Patience the path is steep
and long is the way of heroes
without persecution. But if the pebble
sings in your shoe
tread lightly along the narrow path
of married stone,
in sordina
humming the pebble's tune.

Beauty is the way across
the wide expanse of flowing grey
so very difficult to follow
a fragmentation of the cross
without his crown of thorn
the sceptre falls from parapet
they jump towards the lead
whereon no purple mantle sinks
and laughter explodes like a bomb.

Tragedy is the bridge to cross
when—daring—an aging hand
may not run her fingers
through bristling hair
once soft and golden
and never in her lap
may hold a dead son.

The long spells of fear
hatred and estrangement
will be balanced by errors
and constancy. His is the
pivot and the poetry
each would write for
a beginning to torment.

The rage I've seen, the flare-up
that almost broke his arm
refusing to be sheathed in wool.
But where is the flaw the crack
in the mettle where the demon spawns
the line of devils that mate on scorching crags
their unextinguishable thirst for love?

Is as zero, courage is
without charity in the home
courage is paramount
in destroying affections.

But who will care to mend
mere hearts in a plastic
age where nothing broken
can be put together—

no particle another
attracting? Plastic is
made cheap with rubbish
and similar stuff won't
hold glue nor flame—
is but stench and dwindles.

There

a white lady lay dying
Madonna in ivory—now
dead—without remission
of style and without curtains
at the window to hide from
the passing clouds
                    I gape through
sparkling panes at the empty
moveable aluminum
so obsolete a bed with many
manifold levers and springs.

Here

an old woman better die
alone in her double bed
she needs more space to breathe
than men allow—all lovers
leave—by noon it's demon's hour
and sunset is my dawn.

    I wonder where the sick
    get the word "patient" from
    since we all wait for death
    so very impatiently.

He had never learnt to
recognize the reality
of sin because none there was
in him. But O the flaring
wrath withstood! He doffed the mask
and stood exposed to shield her
from the shame of confessing
her guilt-ridden heart to him.

The snapshot age may soon decline.
They had the meaning, not knowing the place.

A backward longing should not outreach
my youth, but stop at the beginning
of the end of my love where stillness
casts no shadow moving back and forth.

Sever the creating heart
from the rueful mind and bring it
to an even keel, inseparable.
"The arrow has not two points"
he said, and turned it into a poem.

And I will throw my voice in tune with my heart
and meet and mingle with the many voices
of singers alive today. Oh where
where are they? I strain my ear.
No sound, no echo lingers.

Persuasion can be more lethal
than a bullet through the heart
and should not pursue weak game.

Discard, woman, the tear-full quiver
man-made tradition assigned to you.
Artemis shot clean arrows and wept
for one Death stole, not for a strayer
who might oblige, and lie once more
because quicksilver tears scare him
more than a bullet through his head.

When I have wallowed in pain
a little bit
            too long
I go to call
            on St. Peter
and say: should those three gentlemen
(with a grimace) be waiting for me
at your gate when I come
and you, blinded by the beauty
of my soul, let them slip in—
                        God forbid!
            I'll turn
        and stare them
right into hell.

Fearful greedy women surround him.

Husband and wife glued to each
other walk rump to rump
                    it's warmer
her swinging gypsy hips push
three-faced Janus forward, her eyes
are his at the back of his neck
so he can blindly role-
                    play in front
and have his weekend f—
calling it fun (all the while Joy cheer-
ing cheerup drunkenly we'll overcome)
it's not for nothing
the backward gait is called
a carrying wood
                    for the devil.

Scapegoats

In the long high state
                love dwelling made
oblivion of people and places,
names and books of times past
are novelties to one returning
from the close briar patch
where scapegoat with scapegoat
was by Brehon wed until an evil wind
blew their moods asunder.
O hearts so long in high
                esteem and safety kept
within one scallop shell,
on parted wings to blind
moths degraded, heed
joy's brief flame, lest you be burnt.

Jewels

Loneliness goes for jewels
in and out of Tiffany's
when in the swing as low as
42nd trying a double-
take of emeralds and diamond
     RINGS
     are broken and fur alone
cannot hold
     a split head and heart
together.
     GEMS
     teach tears to harden
into topaz, string pearls
and lapis lazuli
around a throbbing neck.
     SORROW'S
     swords are purest silver
in the chest
     begging for candles
               when
loneliness moves on Seraph wings
to the Thrones of Heaven.

Marymagdalen

One of her recurrent fantasies
of childhood was to be an angel
and fly fly from time to time to pause
and comb or stroke her father's blond hair.

When adolescence boiled in her bones
she thought she was a whore knowing nothing
of love or sex. Growing she adopted
roomfuls of children in flesh and blood

placed cots in every corner and looked
upon the lily white diaper field
asking if it were matrimony
she must seek or turn into a Saint

to weep like a Marymagdalen
for non-committed sins at the feet
of a non-existent merciful
man, tear-washing, anointing his hair.

Autumn

I pick my fruit with sun in the eyes
Most of the pears are out of fashion
Have not been poisoned, will neither keep
                                        nor sell.
Shake them into the ditch, hums a wasp
Or I'll sting you. No loss. I gladly
Befriend fat slugs, in winter they feed
                                        the soil.
Every third apple bears bird peckings
Hail-bruise or some ruder compliment
Surely 'tis bad husbandry I say

Precariously perched on a thin bough
Ready to fall for the one rosy and hale
On the highest limb. A butterfly

White whirrs by and I no longer dare
Touch it lest it be her Ladyship's
Very own come to counsel: you reach in vain.

El

As a copperhead rose from the sea
to nestle under your ripply hide
your square root joined the dark tree
in our land bearing flowers in Pisces.

Her slender fists pounded against my mind,
rock-crystal cracked and splintered. She sprung
almond white, a perfect mandala in my eyes.
Dearest, innocence I return to you

Who like to look at a girl's body
naked or hold hands in tender fear.

To the pond no more

She won't have to carefully select
heavy stones to pocket in her coat.
  Though a millstone is
to the mildest god scandal's breastplate,
hurt pride hangs heavy enough upon her
bleeding when he goes the longest way
to cut her
      time short.

Moidl

A woman, thirtyish, which is a lot
for a farmhand in high mountains
where life begins at 5 a.m., aged 5,
to 5 p.m. and 9 through summer solstice
(people die bent and gnarled) attending
into their sixties the "silver mass"
at 4 a.m. during Advent—say this woman
thirtyish at her father's death inherits
a share in her older brother's, and there
are four of them, small farm, has a choice
to be the spinster aunt to seven, she shares
her bed with two already. As sister-
in-law she need no longer work as hard
as a hand, but for pin-money must ask
the penny-pinching, need not greed, big
brother farmer who says: a pig is a feast
and lasts a whole year, in chunks cut into dumplings,
a sheep is a must, one per head, will keep us
in socks and vests, our wealth is the flock
if you spin and dye for the weaver,
                                    our riches
lie in grain and hemp, the cash goes to the State.

                    *

Moidl, thirtyish on the bend, wears
a blue silk apron, pink roses embroidered
and the wax-orange-blossom-wreath on her forehead
carrying the banner of the Virgin guild
for Corpus Christi and Ascension
comes a young rogue, stonemason,
from a neighboring crest. She has a chance.
Hard-luck story, he tasted other people's salt

from the age of seven, once lost a kid
out grazing, herded the goats to the fold
and hid in the barn until fear of a thrashing
was overcome by fear of starving.
"Behold! The kid had been found. No one
had looked for me." The liar. She
knew it yet said, "This is no life
for a man not to call a roof his own."
He yodeled, "Fidelio I am and my whiskers
point to heaven." A king's
pride in the mane and the dancing step.
"If you would but stay, I have a share."
He gave her a brooch. She pricked her nipple
and wept for a year. He spoke to her brother,
and left, crestfallen. She
spoke to her brother and got her share.
Fidelio bought her
                    a copper ring.
She stood for the last time
in her wax-orange-blossom-crown
by towering whiskers, pricks to the sky
in a wedding picture frame of forty years.

                    *

With a bundle and a bale the catholic
creditors moved to a higher plot
seeking their own. Fidelio. The strong.
He played the role, but was not true,
until they were found as Baucis and Philemon,
by Hermes the handsome young wanderer.
Fidelio tells how they began.

"She had thought of lighting a fire
in the field at night when the days were too short

for hoeing and mowing. Sharp as a flint.
Too hard, she worked, too much, had she loved
the land and the animals less
I could now have a roomful of sons,
but she loved animals more—
she lost—broke loose—had she been young..."
Baucis shakes her head. "For a roof of one's own,
and the woods and the meadow, I dote on the dog."
Stroking the flea-ridden bitch, she loses
her heart again to the handsome stranger
who comes and goes. And went away
as sons will go. Her dream of a son.
She lived for one and died for a dream.
The flint-grey hair, the flint-grey skin
as the wax on the orange-blossom-crown
enclosed the kernel of a Virgin Mother kin.
A husk of light, chaff winnowed through the sun
fell to her span without shoes, wearing
but her very own and no teeth.
                    Fidelio weeps
when he finds the denture in a jam jar,
"Cost me my very best cow." Fetch nothing?
Her cow goes to the dentist, and
the blithe shepherd stops at the pub
to pay
        for the wake and a widow's aftermath.

You may well hide
each prickly thing
and shield the child
in an ivory fort
if she's meant to bleed
she'll find the one.

You may brace the man
clothe him in steel
if he was meant to spin
(the gay will tread)
he'll dance down hill
and summersault

to the end of the string

      *

No substitute
        for slowly learning
the difference
        between never going
and never being
        asked to go—"when
are you leaving?"

      *

The child of the native
found no acorn seed
on the $ Mountain
dogs barked and chased her
knee-deep into snow
to grow. To grow?

Rats

A white rat's
fiendish will
(not to
      copulate
with a male
rat but
     to feed
her young) crosses
electric grills,
whereat Time's
black father
will
   fiendishly
make
    the male
forget his plan
to break through
bars. Behind
each friendly
counter
     he can
with science
lie
  in
    state.

Think ill?
It hurts too much.
Think well?
You dope.
Think not at all?
Impossible.
Drown yourself?
In sloth.
      Or hope?
            Straight thinking
            an echo says:
            for there can be no return—
            if once the aching
            fiery path is found—
            to easy
            yokes and yokers.

Where man sees a woman
divine and golden, woman knows
a fiery radiant Benjamin.

His hand can paint his soul
veiled, pure or decadent. If she
attempts to draw the core, diamond

cuts colour and form. Half-
truths are against her commandment.
Truth is in love alone—not art—

in prayer makes self manifest
an angel without feet
without hands wings her soul beyond

space and time, soaring high
over tunnels and mother-caves.
Sisters, let us strive to lead both

mystagogue and scientist where
the idea of love's simplicity
reigns immaculate.

Let stick-in-the-mud play
with vulgar clay and rising dough.
Wafer is the sustenance

at the blood-free Eucharist.

Three Jokers:

Meeting

1. Heaven even now will be jagged
   when you look down from your star box
   into this distrust in Trust you'll pluck
   your copper moustache and red beard
   hair by hair. AOI: all together
   ash blond snow white locks
   rainfall upon us
   wuzzy wuzzy stuff
   brains first rate pulling
   each one over and from under peeee-
   eel
   so slow to open—while the one
   fiery tongue must be held
   inside the loosing gal
   until perhaps she breaks
   loose and the gall flies
   into incomprehensible gloss—o-la-lia
   the glimmer of a match
   to thine eyes.

In the Beanery

2.   the thing to do
here is not to
know but to know
whom to ask hence
no one has to
give the answer
able question
& things are done
with books alone
you write a poem
by looking up
words in the dic
tionaries viz.
  a cowler is a spark arrester
  the monk a prison of burning
thoughts
  and of nuns the fiery glad eye
  if need be it could catch also
  of grampus griseus the jumping
  mind when he loses his grasp on
  orca orca the swift killer

thus sings the sprig
and leaps the kid
losing commas
avoiding dots
never hyphen
catching queries
who grasps the point?

Toccata

3.   Prattle
along
alone does
an aged Fellow
for whom R means
no one to talk to
on 83 Br.
of a Sunday morning
so she watches the gait
and queries the rhythm
of nonexistent lingos
and daddylonglegs'
arti-
    ficial
structure
       build ups
into bagels
(a furren word anyhow)
my Est
     Ling
Mass is over
the tall men walk
with bouquets against their chests
in stiff florist's paper and how
rehearsing on the street the way
to handle fragile stalk and petal
under cover.
        It can't
        be can-
        tos all
        the time
        can it!

Trains no longer run on time
no one is there to wait for you
on the deserted platform
at noon. The bag is heavy
heavier the heart and the feet
drag along the dusty road
though the incline isn't steep
and the yellow house in sight
that never was home.
It's the wavering that draws
the native laden with gifts
to a perfunctory welcome
in a room rich with comfort
minus religion and art.

Distance is not
isolation
      is a gain

in perspective
      to have done
      and to see
its futility
      in perspective
is the gain.

That's the way the road runs
in the mountain—a gradual ascent
from foot to head—stately woman
green, dark red, white—though in places
steep steps have been
hewn into rock or root web underground
she endures wounds deep and wide
for our delight.
The sun is her crown, her ermine the snow,
the Marcher Lords
of a sheep-raising fief
guard the great forests
in the royal domain.
Red is the color
of their Alpine Rose
and a shepherdess heads
his house. She waits for the one
who will never come to pluck
an Edelweiss, gathering
deep blue-throated gentians
for the bridal bed.

Before sleep blesses my tired eyes
and groggy brain, I take refuge in books.
Last night an intruding creature
came fluttering over my head
and I mistook it for a moth,
brushed it aside and gave it
neither room nor attention.
This morning fresh from a long dream
a velvety brown butterfly
lay gasping on the white pillow beside me.
The eyes of Mr. Death—it must have been Him—
gliding down the steel banister
of the Library granite stair visiting
my dream. I shook Him gingerly
and blew Him into the blue.

Now for the poet, he nothing affirmeth, and therefore never lieth

If spoken in soliloquy
my word is void and
hollow the poem? But if
I converse with angels
you do not see? Deny
their existence, I trust
you cannot—for the anagogic
is your theme & Dante
the Master. The difference
between myself and such
as Goethe I guess is he
can drum out poems on
a young girl's back
whereas if my man
turns his back on me
I turn my back and weep.

That rift will always gape at us
two children raised in opposites
a gilded house with ivory
banister landing you on fat
white clouds and a tiger dog
to play with—mine was a mangy
sheep-dog, we raced over damp clods
pelting the ruttish rams back
to their flock and were told
their red pricks were pencils
to write with—so many years
such shame repressed pretending
it was all a fun picnic
with lambs at the Trianon.

When truth is a matter of scandal
should lies stand for good?
Would scandal stick to the doer
or the bearer or the one or t'other
of the unwitting witnesses?
Comes a son of the drunken sailor
looking for the invisible string
the primal plan is strung on.
Slightly dyslexic he mixes Vereker
with Verkehr and weaves new patterns
without seeing the carpet she lies on,
the cover-up patch is her body
so stately, so pure the tyranny
legally established by pen and ink.

Late Lament

I miss you more than thoughts
                          can stretch
and call to you and call
well knowing you are no more
the one who was so dear
                          to me
and I to you
that night's desire bridge
                          two worlds
as magnets drawn to touch mid-air.
From stars you smiled,
your eyes were there, and in the wind
                          your body.
If tempest raged
                with flailing hail
I cried for more
and more well knowing the sun
would shine and dry
                          my body.
Far and near we stood as one
unbreakable wand—so it seemed
until cheap alloy showed for wear.
Yet I miss you still more
and all the more I call
                          into dead air:
Should an infidel ever lie
between unproblematic thighs
oh, White Sister come, stab my eyes
and on your wings carry me in-
to his dream. If love lures not
                          our lives

unto death we are but lonely
phantoms lost.

II

Autumn love, you were born right
in copper forest greening
the buff rose and through flesh
sun-shot your way to clearing-
chambers of the heart whence
a subtle substance rose
to etch our crux in the mind.

Ahi, the scratching pain and pull
inside my eyes lest you escape.
Tear-stars swallowed slowly turn
hard, a pearl's candor nests
in the womb.

      The man is gone
uncomprehending
         stays the child.
Unaided Undine
         went through hell
to be woman
       reborn.

III

Man, beloved and eternal, may the glory
of our sunny days not go waste
the autumn long—come,
cut tendrils smothering an aging
body into rot, let harsh and hard
truths strip us to the core

thrash all vanity to chaff,
lest we be empty pods
and any wind's toy and whip.

Beloved, bleached and dry,
may our bones' friction set
the darkest night aflame
and the cleaving in secret
bring the white light.
                    Requiescat.

Love, lost in the fog of age,
long dreams and separation
truly two ships in the night—
now even Yuletide brings
but few tinsel glitterings.

Love, anchored side by side,
how proud they were at mid-
night, a string of stars entwined
sea and sky in their embrace
to announce the child.

Love, fragile is the word
you used to keep her at bay,
now your skiff no love storm holds,
each must sink alone.

Author's Note:

The present selection is from a bundle of mood-swings, anger, despair, impotence, exorcisms, affections, longing and love spanning almost forty years that could only be expressed in the English language.

The choice is the editor's and follows no strict chronological order. Some poems have previously appeared in print:

"Nostalgia" and "Agro-Dolce," Backwoods Broadsides/
  Chaplet Series, N. 28 Ellsworth, Maine 1997.
"Carol called it comfort food" and "There is something
  in this house," Interim, vol. XII, 1 Spring-Summer
  1993. U. Nevada, Las Vegas.
"Homespun for cousin Mary," A Tribute to Mary
  Barnard; Portland Poetry Festival 1994, Quiet
  Lion Press, Portland, Oregon 1994.
"Marymagdalen," River Styx 5, St. Louis, Missouri 1979.
"Late Lament," Address, Vol. I, no. 2, July-August 1987,
  Keim Publishing, New York.
"Here" and "There," Cairn, vol. xxxi, 1997.

Mary de Rachewiltz has served for over twenty years as Curator of the Ezra Pound Archives, Beinecke Library, Yale University. Fellow of Saybrook College, Yale University, and from 1973 to 1975 Fellow of the Radcliffe Institute (Harvard College, now Mary Bunting Institute). In 1986: Visiting Research Scholar at Kansai University, Osaka, Japan; in 1987: Visiting Professor of English and Canady Center Fellow at the University of Toledo, Ohio. She holds honorary degees from the University of Idaho (1978) and St. Andrews Presbyterian College (1991); she also teaches St. Andrews and Guilford College students at her home, Brunnenburg. Mary has given numerous lectures and poetry readings throughout America, Japan, and Europe. In Italy she has won prizes for her poetry and for her translation of Ezra Pound's *The Cantos*. Besides the works of Ezra Pound, she has done Italian translations of e.e. cummings, Ronald Duncan, Robinson Jeffers, James Laughlin, Denise Levertov, and a few selections of Marianne Moore and H.D. In 1971, Atlantic-Little Brown published her memoir, *Discretions*; while New Directions published the paperback edition in 1975. *Discretions* was published in Italian by Rusconi, Milan in 1972, and the British publication by Faber & Faber in London. Between 1965 and 1996 she has published 5 volumes of poetry with Scheiwiller, Milan and Raffaelli, Rimini.